A Modern Nativity

Four-Week Advent Curriculum & Nativity Play

Table of Contents

Teacher's Guide

This curriculum introduces the season of Advent through the Nativity story while gently exploring themes of empathy, kindness, giving, and understanding homelessness. The goal is to help children connect the story of Jesus's birth to modern-day experiences, fostering a sense of compassion and community.

General Structure:
- **Lesson Duration:** Each lesson is designed to last 30-40 minutes.
- **Components:**
  - **Introduction and Candle Lighting:** Begin with a brief explanation of the Advent theme for the week and light the corresponding Advent candle (battery-operated or symbolic representation for safety).
  - **Storytelling:** Share the traditional and modern versions of the Nativity story to draw connections between biblical events and present-day realities.
  - **Discussion:** Engage children in simple, age-appropriate questions that encourage empathy and understanding.
  - **Activity:** Include a hands-on activity to reinforce the lesson's theme (coloring, drawing, making cards, planning a giving project).
  - **Closing Reflection and Prayer:** Conclude with a reflection, a group discussion, and a short prayer related to the week's theme.

Important Considerations:
- **Create a Welcoming Atmosphere:** Ensure every child feels comfortable and included. Use a friendly, warm tone and make eye contact with all children.
- **Be Sensitive to Different Backgrounds:** Some children may have personal experiences related to the topics discussed. Be prepared to handle questions or emotions with care and provide a nurturing environment.
- **Involve Families:** Encourage children to take their coloring pages and summaries home to share what they've learned with their families, fostering a continued dialogue about empathy and giving.

A Modern Nativity Story

Once in a big, bustling city, there was a couple named Mary and Joseph. They lived a simple life in a small apartment. One day, they received a notice that everyone in the country needed to be registered by the government. This was important, especially for Joseph, who came from a family with a long history.

Mary, who was expecting a baby, knew this journey was necessary. So, they packed their bags and set off to Bethlehem. The city was crowded with people from all over, just like them, who had come to be registered.

After a long journey, Mary and Joseph arrived in Bethlehem. They searched for a place to stay, but every hotel was full, and nobody had room for them. Tired and worried, they finally found a tent under a freeway overpass. It wasn't much, just a tent to shelter them from the night, but it was better than nothing.

That very night, under the twinkling city lights, something wonderful happened – Mary gave birth to a beautiful baby boy! They named him Jesus. Since they didn't have a crib, Mary wrapped Jesus in a soft blanket and laid him gently in a small box they found.

A Modern Nativity Story

In the same city, there were people who didn't have homes and lived on the streets. That night, something extraordinary happened. A bright light shone in the sky, and they heard a voice saying, "Do not be afraid, for I bring you good news of great joy for all the people: in the city, a Savior has been born, who is the Messiah, the Lord."

Curious and amazed, some of the people who lived on the streets went to see this wonder. They found Mary, Joseph, and baby Jesus, just as the voice had described. They were filled with awe and told Mary and Joseph about the message and the light. Mary listened carefully, treasuring these words.

The news of the baby spread, and people came to see him, bringing what little they had – warm blankets, food, and kind smiles. Each visitor left with a feeling of peace and happiness, praising and thanking God for all they had seen and heard.

Mary and Joseph looked at their baby with love and knew that, despite their hardships, they had been blessed with a great gift.

A Modern Nativity: Week 1

Lesson Duration: 30-40 Minutes
Objective: To introduce the traditional Nativity story and gently explore the concept of homelessness in an age-appropriate manner, setting the stage for deeper understanding in the weeks to come.
Materials: Candles, blank paper, crayons, printed coloring pages

Script for Teacher:

1. Introduction to Advent
   a. Teacher Says: **"Hello, everyone! Today, we begin a special time called Advent. Each week, we will light a new candle to help us remember a different part of the Christmas story. This first candle is the Candle of Hope. When we light it, we remember the hope that Jesus brings to the world. We will also talk about how this story might look different if it happened today."**
   b. Light the first candle, symbolizing Hope
2. Reading the Traditional Nativity Story (10 minutes):
   a. Teacher Says: **"As we light this candle, let's think about the story of Jesus's birth and how it brings hope to everyone, no matter where they are or what they need."**
   b. Read: A simple version of the Nativity story, focusing on Mary and Joseph's journey to Bethlehem and the birth of Jesus.
   c. Teacher Says: **"A long time ago, Mary and Joseph went on a long journey to a town called Bethlehem. They were going to have a baby named Jesus and needed to find a place to stay."**
3. Introducing the Concept of Not Having a Home:
   a. Teacher Says: **"Sometimes, like Mary and Joseph, people might go to a new place and can't find a place to stay. They might have to stay somewhere that isn't a house, like a tent or a shelter."**
4. Discussion Questions (5 minutes):
   a. Ask: **"What do you think that would be like?"**
   b. Ask: **"Have you ever seen places in our city where some people might not have homes?"**
   c. Teacher Explains: **"In every city, there are some people who don't have houses. They might sleep in different places. It's important for us to understand and think about everyone in our city."**

5. Activity - Drawing Our City (10-15 minutes):
   a. Materials: Paper, crayons.
   b. Teacher Says: **"Let's draw our city and think about where everyone lives, including places where people without homes might sleep, like shelters, parks, or cars. This helps us see our whole community."**
   c. Encourage discussion about different parts of the city and where people might live.
6. Closing and Reflection (5 minutes):
   a. Teacher Says: **"This Advent, as we get ready for Christmas, we'll learn more about Jesus's story and think about people in our city, like those who don't have a home. We can learn how to be kind and helpful to everyone."**
   b. Teacher Says: **"Let's end today by asking God to show us how we can be kind and helpful to all the people in our city, just like we would want to help Mary and Joseph. We can bow our heads and close our eyes as we talk to God."**
   c. Teacher Prays:
      i. **"Dear God, Thank you for bringing us together today. As we light the candle of Hope this Advent, help us remember Mary and Joseph's journey, and the love and help they received. Teach us to be kind and helpful to our friends, family, and those who have no home. Bless all the people we talked about today, and keep them safe and warm. Fill our hearts with hope and love and help us to share it with everyone we meet. Amen."**

A Modern Nativity: Week 1

Take-Home Page

Today, we introduced the season of Advent and shared the story of Mary and Joseph's journey to Bethlehem. We also began to talk about homelessness by comparing Mary and Joseph's search for a place to stay to the experiences of people today who don't have a home. We encouraged the children to think about ways to show kindness and understanding toward everyone in our community.

A Modern Nativity: Week 2

Lesson Duration: 30-40 Minutes
Objective: To encourage empathy and understanding through a modern retelling of the Nativity story, with a focus on kindness towards those who experience homelessness.
Materials: Candles, cardstock, markers, stickers, and other craft supplies.

Script for Teacher:

1. Introduction and Candle Lighting (5 minutes):
   a. Teacher Says: **"Hello, everyone! Today, for our second week of Advent, we are focusing on peace. When we light the Peace candle, let's think about how we can bring peace to those around us, just like Mary and Joseph found peace in the kindness of others."**
   b. Light the second candle, symbolizing peace

2. Storytelling - Modern Nativity (10 minutes):
   a. Read: The modern version of the Nativity story, focusing on Mary and Joseph's experience with homelessness.
   b. Teacher Says: **"Let's think about how Mary and Joseph might have felt when they were looking for a place to stay. What brought them peace, and how can we help others find peace too?"**

3. Discussion on the Story (10 minutes):
   a. Ask: **"What are some ways people helped Mary and Joseph in the story?"**
   b. Ask: **"Can you think of ways we can help people who don't have a home?"**
   c. Teacher Explains: **"Peace can mean feeling safe, loved, and cared for. We can help bring peace to others by being kind, listening, and helping when we can."**

4. Activity - Kindness Cards (10-15 minutes):
   a. Materials: Cardstock, markers, stickers, and other craft supplies.
   b. Teacher Says: **"Now, we're going to make Kindness Cards. You can create a card for someone you know or for a person in our community who might need a message of kindness and hope."**
   c. Guide the children in making cards, encouraging them to think about messages or drawings that show kindness and support.

A Modern Nativity: Week 2

5. Sharing and Reflection (5-10 minutes):
    a. Teacher Says: "Would anyone like to share their card and tell us what message of kindness they have written or drawn?"
    b. Facilitate a session where students can share their cards and the thoughts behind them, fostering a discussion on empathy and the impact of kind gestures.
6. Closing Thoughts (5 minutes):
    a. Teacher Says: **"Today, we've talked about peace and kindness, and about how even small acts can make a big difference, just like in our story. Let's try to be kind and helpful every day, to everyone we meet."**
7. Closing Activity (Optional):
    a. Teacher Says: **"Let's close our lesson with a circle of kindness. We'll pass around a small object, like a pebble or a ball, and when you hold it, you can say one kind thing you will do this week."**

A Modern Nativity: Week 2

Take-Home Page

This week, we retold the Nativity story in a modern setting to help children understand the concept of homelessness today. We focused on empathy and kindness, discussing how we can help those in need, just as people helped Mary, Joseph, and baby Jesus. The children created "Kindness Cards" with messages of hope and support to share with people in their community.

A Modern Nativity: Week 3

Lesson Duration: 30-40 Minutes
Objective: To teach students about the joy that comes from giving, paralleling the gifts brought to baby Jesus with the act of giving to those in need today, such as individuals in homeless shelters.
Materials: Candles, large poster board or whiteboard, markers

Script for Teacher:
1. Introduction and Candle Lighting (5 minutes):
   a. Teacher Says: **"Good morning, children! Today is a special day in Advent. We get to celebrate joy. We remember how the shepherds and wise men felt great joy when they visited baby Jesus. As we light the joy candle, we will discover the joy of giving by preparing gifts for people who don't have a home."**
   b. Light the third candle, symbolizing joy
2. Review of the Modern Nativity Story (5 minutes):
   a. Read: Re-read the modern story of Mary and Joseph, focusing on their experiences.
   b. Teacher Says: **"Just like Mary and Joseph found a place to stay and were welcomed by others, we can spread joy by welcoming and giving to those in need in our community."**
3. Discussion on Joy and Giving (5 minutes):
   a. Ask: **"How do you feel when you give someone a gift?"**
   b. Ask: **"Can you imagine how the shepherds and wise men felt when they gave their gifts to baby Jesus?"**
   c. Teacher Explains: **"Giving can make our hearts happy. When we give to others, especially those who don't have as much, it can bring them and us a lot of joy."**
4. Introduction to Shelter Giving Project (5 minutes):
   a. Teacher Says: **"This year, our class will experience the joy of giving by collecting gifts for people who don't have a place to live. We'll watch a video about children who, like Mary and Joseph, don't always have a safe place to sleep. Let's watch carefully and think about how we can help people like them."**
   b. Play video: "Parents and Kids Talk About Homelessness" by the National Alliance to End Homelessness at https://youtu.be/CX4TzWdDAFY?si=vQX2HGzgLJIGT52W

A Modern Nativity: Week 3

a. After the video, ask: "What did you notice about how the children in the video felt? What would you want to say to them?"

b. Teacher Says: **"We are going to collect gifts to give to people experiencing homelessness, just like in this video. These gifts will help bring warmth and happiness to people who are like Mary and Joseph, needing a place to stay."**

5. Planning the Shelter Giving Project (10 minutes):

a. Teacher Says: **"Just as people brought gifts to Jesus, we will bring gifts to people who need them in our community. This helps us share the joy of Christmas with everyone. Let's plan what we can give. We'll make a list of gift ideas and how we can collect them. These could be toys, books, or warm clothes."**

b. Brainstorm with the class and create a giving plan on the poster board.

6. Closing and Commitment to Giving (5 minutes):

a. Teacher Says: **"As we prepare to give these gifts, remember how happy it made the wise men and shepherds to give to baby Jesus. We too will feel that happiness when we give to others."**

7. Closing Prayer:

a. Teacher Says: **"Let's say a short prayer for the people who will receive our gifts. May they feel loved and joyful this Christmas."**

b. Teacher Prays: **"Dear God, thank you for teaching us the joy of giving. Help us remember how wonderful it feels to share what we have with others. Bless the gifts we are collecting, and may they bring happiness and comfort to those who need them. Fill our hearts with joy as we give with love, and help us spread that joy to everyone we meet. Amen."**

A Modern Nativity: Week 3

Take-Home Page

In today's lesson, we explored the joy that comes from giving, inspired by the gifts brought to baby Jesus. The children watched a video about children experiencing homelessness and discussed how they could help. We began planning a project to collect and donate gifts to a local shelter, encouraging the children to think about how giving to others brings happiness to everyone.

A Modern Nativity: Week 4

Lesson Duration: 30-40 Minutes
Objective: To teach children about the love inherent in giving, and to engage them in a project that collects and donates items to a local homeless shelter, connecting this act of service to the love and community support shown in the Nativity story.
Materials: Paper, crayons, and stickers.

Script for Teacher:

1. Introduction and Collection Start (5 minutes):
   a. Teacher Says: **"Good morning, friends! Today, in our last week of Advent, our candle represents Love. We're going to show love by giving to others, just like people showed love to baby Jesus long ago. We will start with our collection for the local homeless shelter."**
2. Item Collection and Explanation (10 minutes):
   a. Teacher Says: **"Let's bring up the items we have gathered. Each thing we give, like a pair of socks or a toy, can bring warmth and happiness, just like the stable provided warmth for Mary, Joseph, and baby Jesus."**
3. Activity: Children bring up their collected items and discuss how each one could help someone.
4. Story Connection: Giving as a Sign of Love (5 minutes):
   a. Read: The following passage from the Nativity story about the gifts given to Jesus.
   b. Matthew 2:9-11 (NRSVUE) **"After [the Magi from the east] had heard the king [Herod], they went on their way, and the star that they had seen at its rising went ahead of them until it stopped over the place where the child was. When they saw that the star had stopped, they were overwhelmed with joy. On entering the house, they saw the child with Mary his mother; and they knelt down and paid him homage. Then, opening their treasure chests, they offered him gifts of gold, frankincense, and myrrh."**
   c. Teacher Says: **"The wise men brought gifts out of love. When we give these items, we're also showing our love."**

A Modern Nativity: Week 4

5. Crafting Love Messages (10 minutes):
   a. Materials: Paper, crayons, and stickers.
   b. Teacher Says: **"We will now make special cards to go with our gifts. You can draw a picture or write a friendly message that will make someone smile."**
   c. Guide the children in creating their cards, ensuring each child understands the significance of their message.
6. Reflecting on Love and Giving (5 minutes):
   a. Teacher Says: **"Let's talk about how giving makes us feel. How do you think it makes others feel when they receive these gifts?"**
   b. Facilitate a conversation that allows the children to explore and articulate their feelings about giving and receiving.
7. Commitment to Kindness (5 minutes):
   a. Teacher Says: **"Giving doesn't have to end with Advent. Let's think about how we can keep giving love all year long."**
   b. Activity: Have each child think of one kind act they can do and share it with the class.
8. Blessing the Gifts (5 minutes):
   a. Teacher Says: **"We're going to say a special blessing for the people who will get your wonderful gifts. Let's hope that our gifts and prayers bring them joy and comfort."**
   b. Teacher Prays: **"Dear God, thank you for showing us how to love others. Help us share Your love through our gifts and kindness. Bless those who receive them, and help us spread love to everyone we meet. Amen."**

A Modern Nativity: Week 4

Take-Home Page

For our final Advent lesson, we focused on love and how giving to others is an expression of that love, just like the gifts given to baby Jesus. The children brought in items they collected for a local homeless shelter, made cards with loving messages, and talked about how giving makes us feel. We discussed ways to continue acts of kindness and giving throughout the year, beyond Advent.

A Modern Nativity Play

This short nativity play is designed to be inclusive and adaptable, featuring a few key speaking roles alongside numerous non-speaking parts to ensure that every child can participate with minimal preparation. The script offers flexibility to be adjusted for different group sizes or settings. The play concludes with a rendition of the song "Away in a Manger," re-written with our modern Christmas in mind.

Characters:
- Narrator 1
- Narrator 2
- Mary
- Joseph
- Angel
- Shepherds (children)
- Wise Kids (children)

Props:
- Modern attire for Mary and Joseph, including backpacks
- A small tent
- Skateboards or backpacks for the kids
- Simple gifts (like homemade crafts, diapers, or baby clothes)
- Angel costume

Setting:
- A small tent is up on the stage.
- An AirBNB sign is up with a lockbox.

A MODERN NATIVITY PLAY

NARRATOR 1:

In the city of Redding, Mary and Joseph arrive, part of a census drawing many to this North State town.

(MARY and JOSEPH mime looking for directions on a phone.)

NARRATOR 2:

When they arrived at their Airbnb, it was double-booked. Left with no room, they find a humble spot under the freeway overpass.

(MARY and JOSEPH settle beside the tent.)

(SHEPHERD KIDS are in casual, modern outdoor attire and carry stuffed animals. They enter from stage right, playing and exploring.)

NARRATOR 1:

Nearby, kids roam the streets of Redding, their adventures filled with laughter, unaware of the night's unfolding miracle.

(ANGEL enters from the side, moving towards the kids. A spotlight or flashlight follows ANGEL, illuminating a path through the children.)

ANGEL:

Fear not, for behold, I bring you good tidings of great joy. In this very city, a savior is born.

(SHEPHERD KIDS show awe and curiosity, then exit stage left, whispering among themselves.)

(WISE KIDS enter from stage right, holding simple gifts like stuffed animals, diapers, baby formula, or a onesie.)

Narrator 2:
Drawn by a sense of wonder, children from around Redding come bearing gifts, each one filled with care and love.

WISE KIDS approach the tent, placing their gifts gently near Mary and Joseph.)

(The stage lights soften, focusing on the tent. MARY and JOSEPH look down at a small bundle representing baby Jesus.)

NARRATOR 1:
Beneath the hum of the freeway, in a modest tent, a new hope is born.

(ALL CHARACTERS, including the Shepherds and Wise Kids, gather around the tent to sing Away in an Old Tent.)

Away in an Old Tent

Melody: Away in a Manger

Away in an old tent, no crib for a bed,
The little Lord Jesus, laid down His sweet head.
The stars in the bright sky, their light gently sent,
The little Lord Jesus asleep on cement.

The sounds of the city, the world wide awake,
But little Lord Jesus, no crying he makes.
Be near us, Lord Jesus, In streets where we roam,
and be our dear shelter, wherever is home.

Bless all the dear children, Who wander, unfed,
And guide us to places with warm, loving beds.
Keep watch, gentle Savior, through dark and through light,
And hold all Your children close, safe through the night.

Sample Letter to Adults

Dear Friends and Families,

We are excited to announce that during the Advent season, our children's ministry will be following a special four-week curriculum called A Modern Nativity. This program is designed to help children explore the traditional story of Jesus's birth in a way that connects with their everyday lives, fostering empathy, compassion, and a spirit of giving.

Each week, the children will learn about one of the Advent themes — Hope, Peace, Joy, and Love — through storytelling, discussions, creative activities, and prayers. The curriculum presents the Nativity story both in its traditional form and with a modern perspective, encouraging children to understand the importance of kindness and giving, especially toward those who are in need.

A key part of our Advent activities will be a gift collection project for local individuals and families experiencing homelessness. During Week 3, focused on "The Joy of Giving," the children will be gathering items such as warm clothing, blankets, non-perishable snacks, and simple toiletries. These gifts will be collected on **[specific date]** and donated to a local shelter to help bring comfort and warmth during the holiday season.

We invite you to join us in this special project by discussing the importance of giving with your child and helping them choose an item to donate. Your support will help make this Advent season a meaningful time for both the children and our broader community.

Thank you for being a part of this journey with us. If you have any questions or would like more information, please feel free to contact us.

Wishing you a peaceful Advent season,
[Your Name]

Made in United States
Troutdale, OR
11/20/2024